All by myself

TOYS, PLAY,
TIDY AWAY!

Printed in China

MIX
Paper from
responsible sources
FSC® C104740
www.fsc.org
FSC

Wayland
An imprint of Hachette Children's Group
Part of Hodder & Stoughton
Carmelite House
50 Victoria Embankment
London EC4Y 0DZ

An Hachette UK company
www.hachette.co.uk
www.hachettechildrens.co.uk

All photography by Adam Lawrence except
p1tr, tl & bl, 8, 9, 14, logo and backgrounds: Shutterstock

All by myself

TOYS, PLAY, TIDY AWAY!

WAYLAND
www.waylandbooks.co.uk

4 o'clock — it's tidy up time!

It's time to tidy up now,
And I know just what to do,
I always watch what
my big sister does,
Now I can do it, too!

I love my toys!

Sandwiches and cakes for tea!

I tidy up the tea party;
Cups and plates are put away;
All stacked up in their
special box,
Ready for another day!

I've painted Mum
a lovely picture,
And stuck some
pretty bits with glue,

Then I sort my
clay into colours,
Green, pink,
yellow and blue!

Here comes the train,
Hurtling down the track,
But now it's time to tidy up,
So I put all the pieces back.

TOOT, TOOT!

I gather my plastic buttons,
And sort them by colour and shape....

How many circles
Can you see?

How many triangles
Can you spot?

How many squares
Can you count?

My dinosaurs live on my bedroom shelf, And my cars are kept in a tin...

The dolls go back in the doll's house, And hey presto, a tidy room!

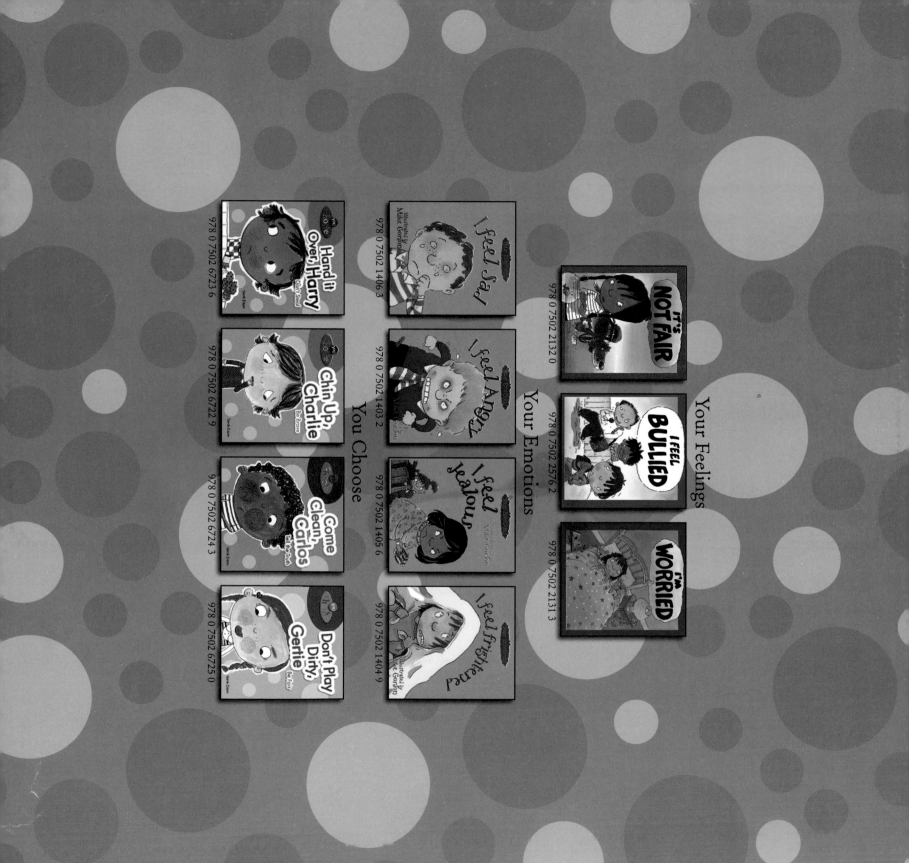

You Choose

Hand it Over, Harry
Don't Shout
978 0 7502 6723 6

Chin Up, Charlie
Be Brave
978 0 7502 6722 9

Come Clean, Carlos
Tell the Truth
978 0 7502 6724 3

Don't Play Dirty, Gertie
Be Fair
978 0 7502 6725 0

Your Emotions

I feel Sad
Illustrated by Mike Gordon
978 0 7502 1406 3

I feel Angry
978 0 7502 1403 2

I feel Jealous
Illustrated by Mike Gordon
978 0 7502 1405 6

I feel Frightened
Illustrated by Mike Gordon
978 0 7502 1404 9

Your Feelings

IT'S NOT FAIR
978 0 7502 2132 0

I FEEL BULLIED
978 0 7502 2576 2

I'M WORRIED
978 0 7502 2131 3